The Phoenix Living Poets

THE SHIVERING SEED

THE SHIVERING
SEED

by

PETER GRUFFYDD

CHATTO AND WINDUS

THE HOGARTH PRESS

1972

Published by
Chatto and Windus Ltd
with The Hogarth Press Ltd
42 William IV Street
London W.C.2

★

Clarke, Irwin & Co. Ltd
Toronto

ISBN 0 7011 1714 1

Distributed in the United States of America
by Wesleyan University Press

ISBN: 0 8195 7032 X

Printed in Great Britain by
William Lewis (Printers) Ltd
Cardiff

To
John F. Danby
and
O. Percy Griffith

Acknowledgements are made to *BBC Wales (Radio 4)*, *The Anglo-Welsh Review*, *Critical Quarterly*, *Triad (The Triskel Press)*, *Poetry Wales*, *Welsh Voices*, *2nd Aeon*, *The London Welshman*, *The Welsh Nation*, *Poems '69*, *The Honest Ulsterman* and *Poet* for poems already printed and broadcast.

The author has received an award from the Arts Council of Great Britain in respect of this work.

Contents

Felling Trees

A child watched the trees fall.
The giant-men's obedient saw,
Golden wood-spray, tall
Crash of a bright arc of axe,
Drew his narrowed eyes.
He smelt the whiff of cut bark
The air's fingers damp
On his ears, blood on his tongue.

The trees scraped the sky to hold
On, hold on to tearing sap: bold
The child stood near the navel roots
Rough from the soil.
In the bleeding moil
He saw the red clay wax
Into dryness in the sun and the butt
Of the tree wave like laughter at him.

Going home he plucked forests
From the earth, ate leaves in wastes
Of frayed wood.
His seven-league axe stood
On his hand like a walking-stick;
His tree-tall saw ripped the world through;
He would chop the thunder when a man.
Woods bent from him where he was quick
With dreams but he did not know why he ran,
Tears splaying, at the shrill call of his mam.

Road Accident

An old man, he walked out
amongst thin drooping rain
onto the road and under the wheels.

Huddled under the sour steel sky
he seemed alive and dozing under
the shock of life gone and skin empty:
the puddled and weeping blood
patterned the folds of his sleeve:
people gathered and stood
as if they, by their very standing
could breathe some willing life
into the lifelong calamities of dying
or dance him down the coloured years
to prink and prance in foam of youth.

But his wife bent and knew ice in the wrist:
the crowd murmured, parted for the stretcher
as if for their own funerals and deaths
then drifted shiftily after the speeding doors
whispering his epitaphs into death's smile.

Thin rain stooped down the street
wheels shushed past the gutters
blurred death's smile into darkness.

Macsen Wledig to the Welsh

Well, I knew they were foolish.
After all, did I not warn them
That my tiny chair held two
Not a whole gaggle of swish
Scholars and a failed people
Whose din breaks my heart in the moo
And baa of their weeping?

Ah my people, in your keeping —
What? A fingerhold on Dafydd,
A conviction of the past, a whorish
Twilight of dreams that, with
Your lack of courage, is seeping
Up your marrow-bones: clownish
How you wail and weep!

Ah my people, can you not keep
Your inheritance amongst you?
The scars, you say, lie deep
And how diligently you reopen the blue
Old wounds, living on your ancient wrongs.
Man, go wail in Annwn and beat gongs
To muddle yourselves more.

I cannot be ashamed again.
That is past now and the ore
(As your scholars say to gain
Understanding with their eyes shut)
Of your loded history is mined away.
Fact that you listen to me shows the hut
Where you hid, the past; turn and face day.

Shepherd

Time had spaced the air with infrequent
Jags of rock and the ground was quick
With boulders and ideas of years past.
A capped and mufflered shepherd and two dogs
Were granite over the wambling sheep.
The peace of eagles brooded on the crags.

Sharply, to the sudden shrill peep
Of the man's tongue, one of the furred blocks
Snaked over the wizened grass and, free
From the weight of time which dog and man felt
In their stiffening bones, harried the leisurely
Sheep, cropping the brown and bents of the hill.

Here the trio were master, but in the lorried
Town they slipped and dodged on the roads, like
Their sheep, chivvied by the oil and noise
Of traffic: what caught them into our time?
Nothing, except the pressure of mortality.

The wind withers, years drown on rain rocks
As the sheep mortgage the dwindling grass.
Over them hoods the blankness of a wasted,
Even though fair and sunset, sky;
And that still vigilance of man and dog.

The Stranger

All things in this fire-flicked
Brasswink and elbow-kept room
Seem anchored in quiet.
Rain slurs the glass and wind lugs
The clothesline in a clog dance.

Keep the wave-walker out of this room
I stack around my soul's sides.
He taps and I am open but would shut
Against him, for flint and wilderness
Are sparked in his eyes and love
That endures the spin and drop of stars.

He knocks on my sand-house,
He enters and smiles.
Terror bulges mind away
To clap doors on his tongue.
He beckons and cries
At my back by the grate
Where I huddle in false calm.
Down crick the clinkers, firefrayed:
Gently in ash pauses, "It is I; be not afraid."

Then tear down the walls to his wind,
Let flint and sand grind in corners
Of darkness, and desert be watered
To green life by his huge love.
Open roofs to the stranger! He brings
The weeping laughter of love to this house.

Poem to Beryl

The heavens, heavy with silver pins,
Winked my way home up the hill.
Our love, strong in doubting winds
Pricked my mind away from their still
Cold beauty; yet I am glad enough
To let these stars and black air
And your love throb out the stuff
Of certitude. I remember the ravens pair,
Though apart, in the mist above Snowdon,
Their sheen flicker before boiling clouds,
Their deep call from the throat, high on
Knife-smelt sky, swinging in casual rounds.
Ah cariad, is it not thus? Paired, though apart,
Sweeping together in tumble-cloud and sundart.

The Long Seam

for Charley Nicholls

I

The old collier, his yoke-like
Shoulders hoisting his short body,
Has gone, his heavy head bent,
Down the long seam to the final face.
He had lingered, rankled with phlegm,
Ripe with humour, and afraid of death,
Yet calm on his old tired legs,
Through his blue eyes, alive and quick,
Now dark as the seam face.

II

Why does the death of one man so split
Words, carve the knit
Ties of family into closer shreds?
A wan feeling like waiting
In stations in the early dawn
Weights the heart fingered
By the cold, reminding hands,
So insolently familiar, of death.
One man's death makes a hole
Through which close threats enter.
The fire blears out and shudders
From the draught of mortality:
Grief, stranger to comfort, lies uneasy
As memory re-casts the man.

III

Once, when young, he trained the black coal,
Arms straight, back curved, fashioned

The dead centuries of crushed trunks,
As sweat trickled to mantling dust.
The grey glint of pick prodded the rock,
Struck, dug down into bowels of coal,
Down through seams seared out,
Thinning down in the jerky lamp:
Conqueror of time in earth's bowels,
Now time's victim in soils alchemy.

Another year he waited with men, workless,
Walked wet roads behind banners,
Rubbed cold hands on his coat,
And waited for a better time.

Then old, he, fashioner of time,
Felt death the rescuer tapping
On the other side of the fall, patient,
Strong, clearing the way to him.
Down long seams of memory his hewed
Life winds, to the ebony face
Which no pick penetrates but death's.

Apart

No birds sing at midnight
    Only the moon mad
Owl snickers in the dark.
    The clock in the park
Touches twelve strokes tenderly.
    Cold time advances
With the night in which you
    And I are apart:
Longing lies buried, like roots
    Struck in sand, limp.
The water of your love distils
    My loneliness into one hour
One hour in which I sleep.
    Dazed by the chill place
In the bed, now stilled
    By the distance
Of your flesh, I forgive sleep
    Forgetting, till light come.

Barracks

At dawn the trumpet trances
The bugler, its cold offences
Brassing sleepers awake.
Black wind and holing sleet
Rake, with wet sharp teeth
Cracked sleep from eyes.
Between the blocks the dawn parade
Begins the dream of a dying man.
In grey, chilled charade
The files waver and answer, clinking
Mugs and coughs mingle with voices.

Huge, soot-flaked walls sag
And belly out beside the square.
In the glum light occasional fags
Glitter, cat's eyes, pair to pair.
The cap, the bolt, the bren, the flare,
All flicker solemnly past drugged
Stares and yawns: worse comes
As the unseen sun rears
Behind the fog; the nodding gears
Of ancient trucks are ground
In unison, and no-one cares.
The pace has your body occupied,
Mind may ponder and skip alone,

Evening — a bored guard breathing
On a loose pane behind the cookhouse,
Scrawling hearts in mist, shifting
On when he hears the sergeant blunder
Round; the heavy air collides with thunder
Lightnings spark and jump
Like kingfishers: the barracks sleep.
Nothing happens, only drunks and defaulters
Ramble back to cell or block
And hours creep round without the clock.

Y Capel

'The Chapel': stamped on your knocker
These words have blinked as beacons
For the ambition of your lost souls.

Good could not have turned a blacker
Hue under the insistent sibilants
Of your yammering pulpiteers.

Yet you held, on brown linoleum
And incense of carbolic,
A few who.knew the laving hands of Jesus.

Now your influence crabs itself in humdrum
Hamlets where the young, sick
And hungry for life, have left you: O, left us!

Would your suffering God forgive the use
Of these once-thronged shells
In the grubby practices of village pump:

Forgive pillaring of community, sauce
For choked pride of men; hells
Of sweating congregations and the slump

Into bafflement; as dreams of deacons
Lord the bench under a minister's
Avid voice, forgive the sour sway

They iced in their country's hearts?
Show them now the soaped silences
Of this tomb-house in the way
Of life. Let us close the false doors.

The Iconoclasts

Cain

I have dug soil
Watched the green grass
Whisper and nod
To red poppies housed
In a lake of green talk.

Under my feet
The dark soil watched me
As I dug down neatly.
The plants I have tended
Talk like the tall grass together.

There is only order here
And I am here.
This is my place
Where my roots are
And the soil crumbles to toil.

That light man, the herdsman,
Has watched me
And thoughts that shine
On my spade's edge
Follow me all day
Through fields of fruit.

Abel

I spy narrowly from the ferns
As the sharp fox crosses the gully.
His stink clouds down the breeze.
My dog whimpers and I silence him.
These beasts are my prey, to hunt

And kill. Favoured of the Lord,
In me there is coiled power.
My red spear halts the boar's rush,
His blood gouts from his neck
As I turn the blade deeper, home;
His squeals gurgle down the haunted woods.
This is my place but I leave his ears for them.
I am here where fear whispers in the grasses
And on the plain where the svelte puma
Skulks on the naked rock rising there,
Watching my fat sheep wander and graze.

I have seen that dark man dig,
Felt the tightness of his body
Poise like a spring and thoughts
That prick between my shoulders
Track me at times in the red forest. ·

Adam

What is there for me to say?
I question Him no longer
But the black fit when worlds
Shake in my brain in my fingers
Comes more often. Cain killed him.
I hunted twice with Abel. .
Small good from such skill and pride.
Cain was more of me . . yet,
Yet I sometimes know, in the garden,
Seeing the dimness of Eve's eyes
And in them a whittled fear,
That we cannot disown him,
That moulded figure cruel as a cat.
Perhaps we came here to rear him,
To witness the start of the end

Which we had begun and to live on.
Thick briars grow in Cain's gardens
And the soil is wet and heavy:
The digging is too much for me now.

Eve

There is nothing for me to do
But watch the bold sunsets spread
Out over the horizon. I am finished.
Their births are finished, their round heads
Pushing at my folding flesh, their fingers
At my nipples, all finished . . but not quite:
I know my daughters will bear down again
And I heave with them and suckle their sons.
Whatever their sons make in the process
Begun by the terrible swoop of Cain's spade
There will be endless birth, pain and death.

Abel, my poor, swift Abel, is white bone
In darkness and damp in the soil;
But his seed is not dead for Cain
Was mine and Adam's and Abel's,
In all of us but not greater than us.
The night filters down and Adam
Walks up from the fields: how old he is.
I know our pleasure was not wrong;
We were only too weak to bear it. Now my hands
Stroke his for comfort and my thin thighs are closed.
The last light goes out in the west and night is here.

Five Love Poems

1 Nightfall

Listen, cariad; the mountains rustle
In the evening and the shrill birds
Are slower in the hedges as time
Runs another night down on us.

Here, in the blessed still air
Of this country, I miss you.
As these hills remember the thump
Of warriors' feet and feel now
The sure, solitary shepherd's tramp,
So I remember your hands until love
Shapes your light out of the gloom.

2 Fire

The fire sputters reluctantly:
Flames lie concealed in heavy coal.
Twist of yellow and snap-red
Split thickening smoke slowly,
With an eating noise.

Fire, gut and spark the coal;
Coal, give and light the fire;
Life, stay your ways here
Where my love combs her hair.

3 *The Red Dress*

Neither ceremony nor the shift
Of squint-eyed time allows
A healing pause for this rift
Or for any human hurt.

You in a red jersey dress
Remind me of someone
Whom I loved and the mess
I made of it all long ago.

Like the sound of grass bending
We sometimes hear the pride
In the heart, quietly rending
The red dress, green heart, the years.

4 *Home*

She has come again
Like a quick bird
To its familiar roost.

Welcome here, your poised
Body, dark hair and eyes
That map our loves.
Most your warm voice
Which touches the nerve
And clothes it once more.

5 Warm

It's warm here, you said.
The heat of sleep, five senses
Folded from bafflement,
The intricate daylight faded.
Some pause in tunnels of night
To remain two bodies, unique
Not grappling, save in dreams,
To fuse bone with heart and life
Into one coherent ball to store
In the head, for future reference.

Sleep then, warm.
I shall watch the windows
Until those wells of blackness
Claim me too.

Icarus

Now you are consummated, Icarus.
Iron bolts with your sons inside
Arrow under the sun, but avoid
The leaping honeycomb of fire
And your brandished agony
Of burnished bones, hung there
Molten in a white pain.

What achievement there is, Daedalus!
Look how your sons have made,
So cunningly, those waxed feathers
Into rivetted steel which soars
Beyond the wide gesture, the hero's psalm,
Yet makes the required safe landing.

Pictures of Diana, Icarus,
She whom you ignored
In your heat-drunk flight,
Reward your father's hands.
The sun, Daedalus, that which
You will never know but sign
Carefully in diagrams, lies still
In your son's twisted bones.

Woman with Child

Swift she caught my finger up
To her side, like the handle of a cup.
Small but heavy with child
She seems to me now gone wild
With secrets chanted by a lost tribe
Round fires, lost in time's bribe
Of history and the lovely curse of breath.

What sure, delving hands have done
And senses have locked from the slum
Of mind rests, rocks, fulcrum'd
Near the lusting world: drummed
From flesh, hot and weary, the child
Sits, spinning the past with mild
Hands, ready to slip like a bright
Wet fish into our dark daylight.

Old Nosey

Like a fleeting crow up the pavement
She goes, headscarf bound like mummy —
Cloth, nose cutting the air for scents,
Coat clapping and dragging to tell
Her of a small chink she missed
Into someone's close-curtained parlour,
Eyes drilling who's watching and who's
Watched, eyes like plump rivets.

Like a squirrel but not so efficient,
Piling speculation, working, glancing,
Noting, quick as a bird to a crumb,
Grab — gone in a dart, stored, noted.
But who watches her . . no-one.
No-one watches: her whole boned life
Is this one street and its carnival
Of drip-dry sins, red as a virgin's
Dreams now harassed to madness
In her insatiable, lonely middleage.

The Cold Road

The fire in the grate is spent,
Its ash clicks and shrinks
Collapsing in little holes, softly.
A dream of corruption traces
A sharp smell of dust in the air.
I am tired and play with thoughts
That lean upon forgiveness.

Now I remember — the thin ash
Drips and makes a pall
For memory — winter air crush
The open shout of heaving lung.
Frost nipped the lad's weaving breath
All along the waving road from school.
Long branches dipped in fastened
Cold, tight-buttoned spring buds
Lay like hidden light on the twigs
Splayed defiance: the boy's dark eyes
Caught the crash of glassy water,
Like tumbling windows, ravelling
Past under the greystone bridge.

The silence of the road, its pattern
Of frost-traced leaves a mosaic
Of chilled clarity, carried a trance
Of awe so deep that he held his breath
In case the trees would snap like ice
And the crackling stream hush like death.

The iron world rang a cold bell,
Its tongue the long-armed frost,
To the clipping run of his feet
And the stilled wonder of his eye
Stayed with the splintering stream.

Webs

Love couched in the crushed grass
That the roadman passes
In the slow wink of early morning.
The webs, skeined with mist,
Hang like life's last tryst
With sleep; the spider's weaving
Tracks the glittering fields.
The labourer's swishing tread breaks
The myriad, sun-caught threads:
These love repairs, patiently patching
The loose fragments of its rounded self,
Making a home for its quick
Flame that spins and delves
Afloat on the tongue's slick,
Its dazed prey fast in the fragile streaks.

Song for my Muses

'Not of father, nor of mother
Was my blood, was my body.'
                Hanes Blodeuwedd. Taliesin.

The still hour holds me
When I can spell simply
The meaning of your love:
Sometimes like hooks in eyes
Then swiftly like a blessing of apples
By sun-shaft and shadow in summer.
I have heard the whisper of your skirt,
The rattle of a rock at your footfall,
Then a cold kiss of air on my nape.
I have been afraid but not cowardly:
Afraid of losing what you give
My coarse tongue to fashion.
Hear a stumbling song, O Cerridwen,
Blodeuwedd of flowers, miracle of flesh —
Poppy head and breasts of primrose
Sheathed in a golden dew of broom —
Sung here and always while words live.

The Litigants

I have watched this rosed sky
Being swallowed by the night —
Starlings gobbling in the twilight,
A suited man dully cutting
The inhibited green of his lawn —
And thought of my countrymen
Mulling over their little sores,
Picking angrily at scabbed resentments,
Filing suits, petitions, cross-petitions
And, in moments of awestruck daring,
Writing anonymous letters to the papers.

O Wales what a bunch of shirtfronts
Embrace you! To enumerate them
Would be a nauseating count of toads,
Of mealy-mouthed weathervanes,
But one or two will suffice here:

Take that unpublic public man,
The schoolmaster, buried under dictates
From deacons and bowed by the blundering
Attentions of whining parents, ambitious
And petty, his chalkraw eyes welded
To the bums of authority and local power;
Then the others — the drivelling poet,
The local doctor venerated as a totem
Is in the rainforests of the savage Amazon,
The flatulent preacher, the ambitious
Parent, filing the panicked mind of a child,
And the professional patriot, raucous
In public, complaisant as an eel in private.
God help you little country, you are fogged
By a horde of litigants, cutting your green throat.

Hill of Arrows

Or Hill of Chariots you are called.
A green rubbled mound like
A baked pudding broken with the bowl
You stick from the sweep of land.

I lie here at your rim and watch
Two flies fuss among the hot lichen
On the stones while a circling wasp,
Tiger among pygmies, makes nearer
And nearer stops towards my hand.

Over there, over the grey-blue water
Is the yellow smear of Merseyside.
Listen and you can hear its tongues
Mixing in the orange air like those yells
Of pain which swathed your sides
With horror in battles long ago.
Down there in the lean shadows
Of the bracken and the hedge
There is a Celtic coffinlid of stone,
Now another stone in the wall.
This is the field of dead men, this hill
Of arrows hunched behind the council houses.

What catalyst can fuse the yawn
Between your tongue and the argument
Finished by plotting, placating
The randy priests in the oak wood,
And by a quick murder or two —
Between my dead, bloodbound world
And its arguments settled with bombs,
Placating the injured god
In its official church and by a quick
Imprisonment or two of its honest men?

33

They are the same world, hill.
My dead world is fused with yours
By the red thread of violence
Through the dark of the years, that rage
Which withered what you built and we still sell.

The smudge of ochre air grows longer
Over Merseyside. Listen, you can hear
Their voices round the corner of the hill;
There, look, they silt slowly over the wide
Valley, like nettles through a fallow field:
This is victory more complete than you have known.
The wasp lies replete on the hot, lichened stone.

Note: The Hill of Arrows, known as The Gop, is an ancient
mound or fort above the village of Trelawnyd, Flint-
shire, Wales.

The Lesson

Not the place of the skulls
    Where three hung,
Not the place of the heart
    Habitually wrung,
Not these learn this lesson:
    It is taught
By the worms in the earth
    I had sought.

Birthday Song

Older soon and no words more
For this darkening love of song.
The glitter gone and only anxiety
Groping in the heaped ore
For the hard diamond of meaning.
No paint to tart up a vision
But a feeling of public derision
As they look at you, naked,
Weeping theatrically in the market.
Yet this remains, the fingers find
What the eye has lost and the ear
Hears the humble music ring
As when a precious vase is struck.
Muse, tongue me a remedy
For I sing no-one but an echo.

Slate Quay: Felinheli

1

This will go too, this curve of shore
Which, bending the tangled Straits,
Looks over at fields that bulge smoothly
Under the folded church of Llanfairisgaer.

Today a brown clout of mist rushes
Over the grey, brawling waters.
The trees bow in anticipation
Curled by the wind's clinical hands
For the sudden drilling rape of rain
On their pale-bellied leaves.

Here, in this village which is asleep
And has not awoken for hundreds of years,
On its blue and grey quayside
Swept of slate piles and inhabited
Now by tatty dogs, lone walkers
The strident gulls and suave
Motor-cruisers, the lives of men
Sing in moist air and the spirit
Of human life wanders, inconsolable,
Pitting a faded emphasis against the end.

2

The small dog which ran, paused, poised
Pissed on a bollard then tracked on swiftly
Has it all his own way.
The bridge waits for the axe
The locks leak and spurt
The arrogant yachts bump the wall
And look as it were not there.

36

An old woman calls the dog which, deaf,
Maps out again its world of odours.

Two times are here but one will conquer
As the sleepwalking people
Twitch obediently to their till's song.

Note: Felinheli is an old slate port, also called Portdinorwic,
on the Caernarfonshire side of the Menai. The port was
once part of the Duff estate.

Llanberis Valley

Snake trails of mist
Vapour through gullies
Scarf thumps from the quarry.
Slate dust spumes
Over blasted slabs,
Lakes glare into intruding cloud.

This is a derelict landscape,
Tourist trap as they call it,
Wrapped contemptuously inward
Trapped in an antiquity
Which has the final ignominy
Of being mere scenery,
Pleasant, majestic, even lived in.
The peoples left, adepts of our age,
Bend towards their lovely earth
Count the summer spoils behind pews,
In midnight blinded shops,
Keep a few native eccentrics
For "The Visitors", eke out
Their obscure patterns beneath
Slavery to cash, cars
And a doomed way of life.

That plane grumbling in the high air
Birds certain of light again
Dogs quieted by mist's dun silence
The stoat still as rusty death
In the hedgerow, the workless
Quarryman gobbing from slate-flat
Lungs, all the torn elements
Of this valley, are borne from habit.

The ground mist crawls up the slopes
Drawn to an unseen disk of heat.

Bald morning now claims the cleft
Dolbadarn castle, some stories
And her face who lifts words from poets
Buried now in blurring light.

Cerridwen

I hear her in these valleys,
Know of her but know her not,
In rowan, hazel, ash and broom
See brown forks of her likeness
Shimmer, glare or vanish,
Remember her move with rippling stride
Across a cuffed field of yellow wheat,
With pressure on my heart hear her
Say, wordless to my wax ears,
Say — what the images, broom
Oak, holly, elm, hawthorn say,
Water lithe through channels,
The bee drunken in pollen perfume —
These things and wordless promise,
Follow me, listen, look, write
And say yourself no more than of me.

My right hand agreed, praised
Through leaves, water, tongued wood.
My left, flaying renegade, sees
Her eat her fat farrow and shrinks.
Both ply through dawn and dusk
Friable seasons of vocables,
In her contours ridden by time
Returned, gone, lost and found,
To make columns of words say
What the heart refuses, the eye
Skips and the day's tongue stutters.

The Guest

A guest in man's house
I tread the wrinkled shore:
Softly the clear moon
Shivers its light on sand
The ever-broken curl
And crash shape of wave,
Blinks a million ground shells.

Gulls and daws shuffle
On the rocks, mewing
In one-eyed sleep:
Above them the salt grass
Grips the black rock.

In the fine shivering dark
I fly up from myself for my soul
Thumps in my throat and my eyes
Are open to the soft quick of life
This moon-webbed evening.

Moth

Your skeletal colours, dust brown
And greys, haired antennae
Like tiny fishbones,
Kept me company tonight.
The lamplight you bask in,
Those strange eyes buttoned
Forward avidly, is no sun
But an artificial ray to light
Poets and other nightworkers
Through the long struggle
Towards dawn and the word.

What do you prove, perfect
In your knowledge of heat,
Singleminded as a fanatic,
Beside my vain fumblings
On this sheet, except
Your uniqueness, one
Of a million such perfections.
How alien we are, I blind
To light, charred by the black
Immensities between us,
You a ghost in lampglow
Poised by the bulb's white core.

Digging Soil

I must feel this soil again
How it clutches with wet grasp
The arches of my boots
Sucks shine into the steel spade
Sinks brown pigment into my fingers
And is, in its volcanic universe
Of feeding life, mine, my blood
And sinew, giver and taker
Mother and whore to my flesh
Dark design of earth's skin
And a dry mystery in summer.

See it take rain until sogged
Grass can swig no more
And the apple tree glistens
With caves of light
Through flaking clouds:
Then soil resumes its drouth
An eternal itch in its myriad wombs.

School Yard

This asphalt is the land
Tumult is its music.
Machine-guns spray
Its dwellers who do not die.
The air is rainbowed
With their stalking dreams.

In corners the private
Concoct their own universe.
With cigarette packets
Stones, bits of stick
The houses are planned.

An echelon of jets
Mayhems through dancers.
In Vietnam their brothers
Crouch from napalm, real
Death, yet these bogeys
Noised from their fears
Are tangible: the eternal
Terrors of childhood
Ghost, witch and bomb.

The Caves
for Gareth

It is a painting by my son,
Bare seven years old.
Red thick arch, blue arc
Of water, falling black rock
Through volcanic red seams.
Outside and around
A brown scowl of brambles,
Tumbling crowns of thorn,
Heavy shapes of yellow toadstools
(Where the fairies live, he said)
Splodged with purple windows,
Finished with a green bulge
Of tree, no trunk, in one
Rung corner, dense and wide
As all the colour that buckles the paper.
I wished I had its complete authority,
Its flat, gaily true vision,
Not what I remembered . . . . .

The old lead-mine shaft,
Drilled entrance, scree of stones
Clay and grappling bushes
Among still trees, the dark
Rock gullet and we, a three-year
Child and would-be man,
Peeping dubiously down.

Who lives here?
Puff and Bowlen live here.
Right inside there?
The dim passage bored straight
Into the Clwydian hill.

Yes, far away down there.
And the fairies?
Sometimes . . Yes, the fairies, down there.
Can we go in?
Well —
They won't be cross, y'know.

God knows, you should know
More than I, your world
A truer growth than my adult
Compound of fears, cynicisms
And failures. So we stepped
Our way in, child and man.
Struck matches spat in dampness,
The stream — Why is there water? —
Tinkled like a whore's anklet.
You didn't know I sought your hand.
Thirty feet in the galleries
Spiked off into crawling dark,
A pool opened its pitch eye
Deep below, water dribbled
Through cold rock, spidered
In my hair, lived in cracks
And limed bumps of roof.
I looked back to the entrance's
White welcome, you gazed
Through those nets of darkness.
Are Puff and Bowlen home?
They are out; they come here teatime.
Is it teatime yet? Not now.
And if they had come then, if . . .
Puff is a dragon.
Yes, and Bowlen a prince.
Bowlen and Puff are friends.
They are; let's go out now.

Your little pale face lit
Our way to the mouth.

I was never so glad of air.
Sky and leaves and sun a shout
Of light: I wasn't afraid, dad,
Was I? Air and light and —
No: nor am I, now.

All the way home you talked
Of dragon and prince, yelled
Them at dull bullocks we followed
Through the fields to the grey stile.
I had to concoct another story
That night; a sunlit one
To plug that dark, inimical
Shaft of stone in my heart.
The water dripped in my mind
For three years until your paint
Released it here: Puff's cave,
You said, and that's where we went,
Didn't we? To the mountain,
When I was a very small boy.

I remember, I said, the still plink
Of the water ceasing its wear.
We understood. The wild aria
Of a storm-thrush trembled
The windowpanes: it mattered
Not whether it was light or dark.

Woman Sewing

I suppose your sewing is surer
Than all my efforts to hold
Images together, the threads
Of intuition parting
Like rotted hawsers, my ships
Adrift bobbing onto the reefs.

Yet what you do is agelong.
How many women, muttering,
Have sat thus, patterning
A coloured dress or patching
A hole in a shirt, the quiet
Chack of machine or thimble a pulse
For peace in a restless room.

Our activities are different though:
I want the truth naked in all weather
Whereas your probing fingers cover
The shivering seed of man in shirt or shroud.